MATTHEW HENSON
POLAR ADVENTURER

MATTHEW HENSON
POLAR ADVENTURER

by Jean Kinney Williams

Franklin Watts
New York / Chicago / London / Toronto / Sydney
A First Book

Quotations used in this book are from
Matthew Henson's autobiography A Negro Explorer
at the North Pole, *New York: Frederick A. Stokes, 1912.*

Cover illustration by Amy Wasserman
Cover map copyright © North Wind Picture Archives, Alfred, Me.
Cover photograph copyright © Peary-MacMillan Arctic Museum, Bowdoin College

Photographs copyright ©: University of Michigan Library, Ann Arbor, Mi.: pp. 2, 10;
Stock Montage/Historical Pictures Service: p. 8; North Wind Picture Archives: pp. 13,
15, 18, 23, 47; Dartmouth College Library, Hanover, N. H.: pp. 16, 30, 32, 38, 46, 52;
The Bettmann Archive: pp. 17, 33, 36, 40; Photo Researchers, Inc.: pp. 21 (Simon
Fraser/SPL), 25 (George Holton), 50 (Mary Evans Picture Library); Robert E.
Peary/National Geographic Society: pp. 24, 27; Peary-MacMillan Arctic Museum,
Bowdoin College: p. 44; UPI/Bettmann: pp. 55, 56, 58.

Library of Congress Cataloging-in-Publication Data

Williams, Jean Kinney.
Matthew Henson, polar adventurer / by Jean Kinney Williams.
p. cm. — (A First book)
Includes bibliographical references and index.
ISBN 0-531-20006-X
1. *Henson, Matthew Alexander, 1866–1955—Juvenile literature. 2. Afro-American*
explorers—United States—Biography—Juvenile literature. 3. North Pole—Juvenile
literature. [1. Henson, Matthew Alexander, 1866–1955. 2. Explorers. 3. Afro-
Americans—Biography. 4. North Pole.] I. Title. II. Series.
G635.H4W55 1994
919.804—dc20   *93-6101*
[B]   CIP AC

CONTENTS

MATTHEW HENSON
POLAR ADVENTURER

*Commander Robert E. Peary spent eighteen years
exploring in the Arctic, always with the goal of being
the first person to reach the North Pole.*

F O R E W O R D
TO A
REMARKABLE
STORY

One hundred years ago, the ice caps over the North and South poles were unexplored. Some countries, including the United States, sent expeditions north to Greenland to learn more about that part of the world. The fierce climate doomed many of those expeditions to failure.

But some couldn't resist the challenge, including Robert Peary, who worked for the United States Navy. He carved and won a place in history when, after many attempts, he planted the American flag at the North Pole in 1909. But he might have accomplished far less if not for his African-American assistant, Matthew Henson, of whom Peary once said: "I can't get along without him."

This is the story of Henson's last trip north, remarkable not just for what he accomplished as a black man at the turn of the century, but as compared to any person in any era.

Peary and Henson during
their trip to Central America

10

CHAPTER ONE
FROM
NICARAGUA
TO THE
NORTH POLE

It was a blistering hot July day in 1908 when a ship named the *Roosevelt* chugged away from New York City, bound for the icy waters of the Arctic Ocean. As Matthew Henson gazed from the ship at the soft green hills of Long Island, the rocky, icy coast of Greenland for which the ship was headed seemed distant and harsh.

For Henson and Robert Peary, the journey was familiar, taken several times during the twenty years that they had worked together as assistant and explorer, respectively. Both knew it would have to be their last attempt to reach the North Pole.

Peary, a civilian navy officer, was fifty-two years old. Henson was almost forty-two. Their work in the Arctic was too demanding to continue making trips there. This time, Peary decided, they must reach the North Pole or die trying.

Henson's commitment to that goal was no less than Peary's. Hard work and adventure had been part of his life since he was thirteen.

Born August 8, 1866, on his parents' farm in Maryland, Henson and his family moved to Washington, D.C., when he was a baby. When his mother died, he lived with an uncle, going to school until he was thirteen. Then, his uncle no longer could support him.

Matt found work at a restaurant, sleeping there at night. One customer, a sailor, told the young boy tales of life aboard a sailing ship, and Matt wanted to try it, too. He left the security of his restaurant job and walked 40 miles (64 km) to the port at Baltimore, Maryland. Standing by a dock, he noticed a beautiful ship called the *Katie Hines*. The ship's captain, a leather-skinned, white-haired man named Childs, noticed Matt, who found the courage to approach him.

"Do you need a cabin boy, sir?" Matt asked.

"And who might you be?" Childs replied patiently, studying the raggedy boy who seemed to come from nowhere.

"I'm Matthew Alexander Henson, from Washington."

"How did you get all the way to Baltimore, Matthew Henson? How old are you?"

"I'll be fourteen soon. I walked here to work on a ship. I don't have any family." Matt spoke matter-of-factly, with no trace of self-pity. Childs, admiring Matt's determination, signed him up as cabin boy.

Matt worked hard for Childs, and over the years they enjoyed almost a father-son relationship. The captain taught the boy about history, geography, and navigation, while Matt saw the world, sailing to Asia, Africa, and Europe.

Matt's good fortune ended in 1885 when Childs became ill and died. Matt found work aboard a fishing schooner, where he learned the painful lesson that skin color often mattered more than ability. Disgusted, he quit the schooner and traveled around the United States

The sailing master was often exposed to harsh wind, cold, and saltwater during journeys.

before moving to Boston, where he looked for the type of work he had learned aboard ship, such as carpentry or mechanics. But trade unions, which controlled who could work in these fields, wouldn't accept black people as members.

Matt had various jobs in the northeast and landed back in Washington D.C., taking a job in a hat shop. The work was dull, but his employment there brought him to a turning point in his life.

One day, a man entered the store to buy a sun helmet. As he tried one on, he asked Mr. Steinmetz, Matt's employer, if he knew of anyone who could accompany him to Nicaragua, where he would be working on an engineering project for the United States government. Knowing of Matt's traveling experience, Steinmetz introduced him to the man. "Matt, this is Lieutenant Robert Peary. He needs a manservant to assist him in Nicaragua."

Matt liked Peary's straightforward manner and instinctively trusted him. He and Peary shook hands in agreement, though neither might have guessed that this would be the first of many trips they would make together, beginning in the jungles of Nicaragua and finishing on the ice cap of the Arctic Ocean.

* * *

From the start of this 1908 voyage, Henson liked the enthusiasm of the "tenderfeet," Peary's nickname for

Commander Peary and his sailing
master aboard the Roosevelt

men on their first expedition. They were George Borup, a recent college graduate; John Goodsell, a physician; and Donald MacMillan, a college instructor who also would become an Arctic explorer. MacMillan admired Henson's strength and capability, and the two men became good friends.

Returning for a second trip were also Bob Bartlett, who was captain of the *Roosevelt*, and Ross Marvin, another college instructor. They had been along on the 1906 expedition, when the less experienced Peary and

Ross Marvin, a key member of Peary's
last two expeditions, tragically drowned
in the icy water of the Arctic Ocean.

his men had found that they were no match for the ter-
rible storms and broken ice on the frozen Arctic Sea.
Turning back, the explorers were fortunate to return
alive. But Marvin and Bartlett were hard workers, and
Henson was glad to have them along. As for Peary,
Henson described him in his book, *A Negro Explorer at
the North Pole*, as walking "with a peculiar slide-like
stride," having lost several frostbitten toes in an earlier

16

The Roosevelt's *crew had much work to do
to keep the ship running smoothly on its voyages.*

expedition. "He has a voice clear and loud, and words never fail him."

The *Roosevelt* rode up the East River, sent off by cheers from other boat skippers. The next day, the ship stopped long enough to receive President Theodore Roosevelt, for whom the ship had been named. He was fascinated by Peary's Arctic equipment. "How I should like to go!" Roosevelt exclaimed. "Good luck!"

As the ship made its way along the coast of Canada, Henson thought of his young wife, Lucy, whom he had married just a few years earlier. He hoped that the next time she heard about him it would be good news that would make her happy and proud.

The Inuits' hard-working dogs
were an essential part
of Peary's expeditions.

CHAPTER TWO

INUIT FRIENDS

Once the expedition reached the Arctic, what was the best way to get to the North Pole? One man wrote to Peary wondering why he didn't drive an automobile there. Like most Americans, the letter writer didn't know much about the ice cap covering the Arctic Ocean. It sometimes had ridges of ice as tall as houses, or large areas of open water, called leads, that were impossible to cross until they refroze.

Henson and Peary had learned that the Inuit (until recent times called Eskimo) way was best for traveling in the Arctic. The Inuits used dogs to pull sleds full of equipment and built igloos to sleep in. The Inuit men traded the best sled dogs to Peary and Henson in return for items such as guns and bullets for hunting. The Inuit women made them fur clothing in exchange for metal needles, cooking pots, and other items that the Inuits considered treasures.

Peary treated them fairly over the years, and they

respected him, but it was Henson they truly loved. When Peary and Henson first approached the brown-skinned Inuits for help and supplies in 1891, they saw Matt's own dark skin and cried "Inuit!" They thought Matt was one of them.

Henson, too, was very fond of them. Among all the people he had met traveling around the world, Matt called the Inuits the "best-natured people on earth, with no bad habits of their own." Their children were "much loved, never scolded or punished, and are not spoiled."

Many Inuits, afraid to travel far from their small villages, refused to accompany Henson and Peary. But some were willing to do anything they were asked. When, in July 1908, a group of Inuits at Cape York Bay saw the *Roosevelt* coming, "They remembered us, and were dancing up and down the shore, and waving to us in welcome," Henson later wrote in his book.

The Inuits were an unusual sight, with their long black hair and animal-skin clothing. But, like Henson, most of the expedition members enjoyed these friendly people.

They also found Greenland strikingly beautiful, as the ship caught sight of enormous icebergs jutting out of the sea against a bright blue sky. There were colorful mosses growing on the rocks, and wildflowers sprouting from the grassy patches near the coast.

A place of grand beauty, Greenland was like another

*Ice is always a part of Greenland's
coastal scenery, even during
the colorful summer months.*

world. But for the next twelve months it would be
home, and the Inuits would be constant companions to
the men aboard the *Roosevelt*.

CHAPTER THREE

GREENLAND

Once in Greenland, Henson got to work, trading with the natives for things the expedition would need, such as dogs and animal skins. He also decided which native people to hire for the expedition. One man named Seeglo, for example, was offered two hunting rifles and ammunition in exchange for his pack of sled dogs and his assistance on the expedition. Seeglo readily agreed.

Henson also hunted for the dogs' winter food supply as the *Roosevelt* traveled up the coast of Greenland, taking aboard Inuit families. Another ship, the *Erik*, followed. It was full of coal for the *Roosevelt*'s hungry engines and whale meat for the hungry dogs.

As they anchored at Etah, the northernmost inhabited point of western Greenland, the *Roosevelt* was crammed with coal, people, yelping dogs, and literally tons of rotting whale meat. But everything was rearranged to make room for more coal from the *Erik* so that the *Roosevelt* could continue alone.

By mid-August it was time to go north again to

Cape Sheridan, where the *Roosevelt* and all on board it would spend the winter locked in the frozen sea. After a blinding snowstorm, the powerful ship was on its way, "with all the dogs a-howling, the whistle tooting, and the crew and members cheering," Henson would later recall in his book.

For three weeks, the *Roosevelt* plowed through the icy channels leading to Cape Sheridan, and arrived there September 5. During that time, Henson built sleds and, as he put it, had a "steady job carpentering, also interpreting [he was fluent in the Inuit language], barbering, tailoring, dog-training, and chasing Esquimos out of my quarters."

The icebound Erik *in the Smith Sound*

The Roosevelt *carried almost 250 dogs in addition to tons of food, coal, whale meat, and, of course, dozens of people.*

The long, sunless Arctic night was approaching. Henson wrote in his journal that "... in spite of my years of experience, I can never get used to ... the black darkness of the sky, the stars twinkling above, and hour after hour going by with no sunlight."

*In the summer, the sun is visible all
day in the Arctic even at midnight.
In the winter, it disappears altogether.*

Peary helped combat the men's winter blues by keeping them busy. They hunted, learned from Matt how to drive a dogsled, conducted scientific research, and carried supplies to Cape Columbia, the point on Ellesmere Island from which the expedition would depart in February.

But Matt saw humor, too, in life aboard the ship. He wrote that Peary expected all expedition members to bathe at least once a week, a custom that was new to the Inuits but one to which they took eagerly, sometimes even hopping into a big pot of water kept in the kitchen that was to be used for cooking.

For quiet moments there were plenty of books on

board. Henson read Charles Dickens, Rudyard Kipling, and poet Thomas Hood, as well as the Holy Bible. "But," he admitted, "mostly I had rougher things than reading to do."

Finally, it was time to go to Cape Columbia. On February 18, 1909, Henson left the comfort of the ship, aware, as always, of the possibility that he might never return. He traveled with three Inuits; each of their four sleds carried around 250 pounds (113 kg) of supplies, such as pemmican, biscuits, tea, and alcohol.

Pemmican was a canned mixture of meat and fruit. There was one type of this mixture for the men and another for the dogs. The men would have biscuits with their pemmican and carried alcohol along to heat small stoves on which they brewed pots of hot tea.

Henson's party arrived at Cape Columbia on February 22. The air was so cold that day that all of their faces were covered with frost. In less than an hour, the party had their igloo built. Made from blocks of packed snow, igloos didn't offer much warmth, but provided protection from wind and snow.

The clothing made by the Inuit women would be worn when the trip for the pole began. Besides fur jackets, each man had a pair of polar-bearskin pants and boots, a deerskin shirt, and socks made from hare skin. Henson showed newcomers that the best way to keep their feet warm was to stuff grass into their boots.

Peary planned to reach the pole with a type of relay

Henson, holding a baby musk ox and
wearing fur clothing made by Inuit women

system: one party of men would pioneer the route and make a trail, building an igloo at the end of their march. Then the remaining parties would have a trail to follow and an igloo to stay in at the day's end, as well as having improved the trail along the way.

Eventually, one or two parties at a time would be sent back so that as the trail progressed, fewer supplies would be needed. Finally, only Peary and a few others would be left for the last leg of the trip to the pole. None of the men knew yet who would be chosen to go with Peary.

On February 28, Peary arrived at the cluster of igloos, shouting orders. Bartlett and Borup loaded their supplies onto their sled and headed north onto the ice of the Arctic Ocean. Another expedition for the North Pole had begun.

By 6 A.M. on March 1, Henson's party was ready for Peary's "Forward! March!"

"From now on," Henson wrote, "it was keep going . . . sometimes in the face of storms and wind that it is impossible for you to imagine." But, as he had always done in the past, Henson kept on going.

CHAPTER FOUR
ICE
AND
DELAYS

The air was colder than –50° F (–45.6°C) the morning Henson and his Inuit companions urged their dog teams forward onto the ice to follow Bartlett's trail. When the ice was smooth, the men would hop onto the back of the sleds. The rest of the time they ran along behind the sleds, holding on to handles that were attached to the back.

"After leaving the land ice-foot, the trail plunged into ice so rough that we had to use pickaxes to make a pathway," Henson wrote. It wasn't long before Henson's sled split. "'Number one,' said I to myself."

He bored new holes in the sled, then took off his mittens to thread the pieces back together. When his fingers began to freeze, he put them under his armpits for warmth. Then he hurried his dog team along to catch up with the rest of the party.

Eventually, the group reached the igloo Bartlett had slept in earlier, 12 miles (20 km) from land. "Our breath was frozen to our hoods of fur and our cheeks and noses

*The Inuit made igloos by cutting
blocks of packed snow when they were
traveling away from their homes.*

frozen," Henson wrote. It was too cold for anyone to sleep much that night. In the morning, they found that their breakfast pemmican had frozen and cut the insides of their mouths as they ate.

That day brought more rough ice that required the use of pickaxes. Many hours, but only 7 miles (12 km) later, they reached open water, or leads. These breaks in the ice were caused either by warming temperatures or sometimes by the movement of the water underneath. Heading west, Henson's party found new ice on which to cross. The next day, the ice floes around them splintered with a thunderous cracking.

On the fourth day, 45 miles (75 km) from land, Henson's group plowed through more deep snow, until they reached thick floes of smooth bluish ice, which made traveling quick and much easier. But soon they caught up with Bartlett's party, which had been forced to stop by another lead of open water.

This lead, called the Big Lead, was a fourth of a mile across, and unpassable to either the east or west. No one could advance until it froze over again. The next day, a clear sky allowed the first glimpse of the sun at noon, but ahead was only the icy black water of the Arctic Ocean. Peary sent MacMillan back to land for more supplies, and the other men kept busy repairing sleds, drying out their fur clothing over oil lamps, and rearranging the sled loads.

Two days later, MacMillan returned and told Henson that his heel was painfully frozen. Henson advised him to tell Peary, but MacMillan wanted to keep going and decided to keep it a secret, a decision for which Henson admired him. "His first trip to this forsaken region," Henson wrote of MacMillan, "yet he wakes up from his sleep with a smile on his face and a question as to how a nice, large, juicy steak would go about now." MacMillan also helped Henson keep up the Inuits' morale; they were sure the ice devil was keeping the lead open. MacMillan organized games for them to play, and the winners of boxing, wrestling, or thumb-pulling matches were promised prizes from the ship after the expedition.

The expedition began with several parties
of three or four sleds each. Eventually, however,
only one party would go all the way to the Pole.

 32

*Travel could be very slow
through the rough ice.*

The delay frustrated Peary, too. Precious supplies were being consumed with no telling how long it would last. Their last trip onto the polar sea, in 1906, was a failure primarily because of the Big Lead. Would this expedition be doomed, as well?

Finally, on March 11, the temperature dropped to −40°F (−40°C), and the lead froze over. Heading north again, the expedition crossed several leads, always on thin, new ice. Sometimes they had to climb over enormous pressure ridges that were formed as the ice froze back together.

There were more leads the next day, but all could be crossed. By March 13, the temperature fell to −53° F (−47°C), but their hard work, combined with increasing sunshine each day, kept the men warm.

The next day would be the last northward march for MacMillan, who finally showed Peary his frozen feet. Peary had no choice but to send him back, along with Dr. Goodsell. Peary continued to put his relay system into action by sending parties back and paring down his expedition. MacMillan and Goodsell wouldn't be going all the way to the pole, but who would?

The next day, Henson was ordered to pioneer the trail.

CHAPTER FIVE
TRAILBLAZING
AND
VICTORY

Travel was slow as Henson's party broke the trail. Detours around small leads and travel through deep snow, in addition to carrying 550-pound (250-kg) sled loads, made progress difficult. After putting in a twelve-hour day, Henson was exhausted.

The following days brought more leads, crossed either on thin ice or maneuvered by going from one broken ice floe to another. The wind, whipping through any opening in the men's clothing, Henson said, would "pierce us with the force of driving needles. Our hoods froze to our growing beards."

The group crossed pressure ridges as high as 60 feet (18 m). Henson would cut a trail over the ridges and then come back for the sleds; it took all the men's strength to push the sleds up the incline. And going down the other side was worse. One sled slipped from their grasp, smashing at the bottom of the ridge. The dogs, looking on, shook with fright. It took Henson an hour to fix the sled.

Matthew Henson's nickname
among the Inuit was "Miy Paluk,"
which meant "beloved Matthew."

That night, March 19, Peary told Henson to select the best dogs from his teams. The other dogs would return with Borup after the next day's march.

Bartlett and Henson each blazed new trails for the next few days with Marvin and Peary about twelve hours behind them. Because of their position and the time of year, the sun shone half of each day now, and nighttime looked more like twilight. To figure their location, Peary used instruments to measure the sun's angle over the horizon.

Smooth ice allowed Henson and Bartlett long days of trailblazing. On March 25, Peary told Henson to spend the next day sorting out the best dogs and rearranging the sled loads. Marvin, his feet badly frozen, was turning back.

Henson, relieved that he was still part of the expedition, found his Bible while rearranging the sled. With weeks of uncertainty ahead of them, he sought comfort that night in his igloo reading some of the passages.

March 27 dawned cold and sunny. Before Marvin turned back, Peary shook his hand, saying, "Be careful of the leads, my boy!" In his good-bye to Henson, Marvin "advised me to keep on, and hoped for our success," Henson would later write. But "my good, kind friend was never to see us again." Henson and Peary later learned that Marvin never made it back.

Now 240 miles (386 km) from land, they were near the same point where Peary had turned back three years

Arctic explorers, including Peary,
considered the dogs from Greenland's
Smith Sound to be the best available.

earlier. This time, though, everyone was in good shape with plenty of supplies remaining. But the expedition always met new tests of endurance.

On March 28, Henson and Peary arrived at Bartlett's campsite and built igloos about 100 feet (31 m) away from Bartlett so that they wouldn't disturb his rest. While all slept, a lead opened up between the two camps.

All the men rushed out from their igloos to see ice floes moving in every direction. Bartlett's party was on one ice floe, which slowly drifted toward the others. Bartlett's men and dogs quickly crossed over to join the rest of the party just in time to see their floe disappear into the darkness.

On April 1, the dogs were rearranged for the last time: Bartlett's party was going back. He gave the others a cheery "Good-bye! Good luck!" After having worked so hard, Bartlett masked his disappointment at turning back just 130 miles (209 km) short of the North Pole.

For Henson, twenty years of work with Peary, many of them spent striving to reach the North Pole, were coming to the finish he had so hoped for. "Commander Peary and I were alone (save for the four Esquimos), the same as we had been so often in the past.... We knew without speaking that the time had come for us to demonstrate that we were the men who, it had been ordained, should unlock the door which held the mystery of the Arctic."

Now impatient, Peary wanted to cover 125 miles (201 km) in five days. "We marched and marched, falling down in our tracks repeatedly," Henson wrote. On one occasion, their impatience almost cost them their lives: Both Henson and Peary fell into the sea while crossing thin ice. Henson was saved only when his good friend Ootah grabbed his coat by the neck with one hand while keeping control of the dog team with the other. Catching up with Peary's party, Henson's group found that their leader was being helped out of the water by his Inuit companions as well.

On April 5, Peary estimated they were 35 miles (56 km) from the pole. Leaving before midnight, they marched 15 miles (25 km), took a break for dinner and

Peary took this photograph at
the top of the world: the North Pole!

40

hot tea, and traveled another 15 miles (25 km). With that, Peary figured on a compass they were at 89° 57' latitude, or 3 miles (4.8 km) from their destination of 90°: the top of the world. Although their goal of so many years was finally accomplished, Peary and Henson had no energy to celebrate.

Igloos were built, dinner was eaten, the dogs were fed a double ration of food, and everyone slept for a few hours. Awakening the next day, April 6, Peary was thoughtfully quiet. He took out the flags he had been carrying on his expeditions for years. Fastening the United States flag to a pole, he placed it atop his igloo.

"A thrill of patriotism ran through me," Henson said of that moment. He led the four remaining Inuits in a round of cheers, although to them, arriving at this forsaken spot after risking their lives to get there certainly didn't seem anything to cheer about.

Henson couldn't help but take pride in his own achievement: "Another world's accomplishment was done and finished," he wrote. "I felt all that it was possible for me to feel."

CHAPTER SIX
THE
LAST VOYAGE
HOME

Peary and Henson spent little time thinking about their achievement. Spring was coming, and they needed to get off the ice before it became too unpredictable. Peary planned each day's march to be twice as long as usual until land was reached making the journey ahead of them even harder.

Luck was with them on this return trip, their last over the Arctic Ocean. The trail they had made earlier was still visible, and they had plenty of food as well as ready-made igloos awaiting them at the end of each march. The Big Lead was frozen, and they stayed in the same igloo campsite where they'd spent several frustrating days a few weeks earlier. As they finished their meal and prepared to leave, the lead opened up once again, this time behind them!

Ten days of double marches, sometimes covering 45

miles (72 km) at a time and traveling into the sun, left both the dogs and men exhausted. But by April 19, the mountains of Grant Land were visible. Just before midnight, on April 22, the party reached land, and the Inuit whooped and hollered with excitement. Cape Columbia was reached about six hours later.

It had been about seventeen days since they had left the North Pole — "such a seventeen days of haste, toil, and misery as cannot be comprehended," Henson later wrote. "The winning of the North Pole was a fight with nature."

Their fight with nature over, Peary and Henson figured they had won fame and recognition. But for now, just being alive after planting the American flag at the North Pole was reward enough.

After two days spent mostly sleeping at Cape Columbia, Peary left for Cape Sheridan, followed by Henson's party a few hours later. Approaching the *Roosevelt*, Henson could smell coffee brewing and tobacco. Then "a party of the ship's crew came running out to meet us," he wrote. He felt "overjoyed to find myself once more safe among friends. . . . I did not realize that some were missing."

Peary and Henson learned upon returning that Ross Marvin had drowned in the Arctic Ocean. He had fallen through thin ice over the Big Lead, said his Inuit companions, who were too far behind him to help in time.

The Roosevelt *begins the
long journey south toward home.*

Losing Marvin was heartbreaking for all the expedition members, and a memorial cairn of stones facing the sea was erected in their lost companion's honor.

After his first deep sleep in weeks, Henson awoke to devour a wonderful meal cooked especially for him, and then washed off weeks' worth of grime in a long, hot bath. After several days of rest and good food, he began to feel like himself again. But Marvin's death haunted him during this period of recovery, as it did the others. Bartlett was quiet and spent much time in his cabin. Peary didn't speak to Henson for three weeks after the return.

The ship was scrubbed clean, and on July 18 it headed south, stopping at Inuit villages along the way to return families to their homes. Expedition members hunted for the Inuit's winter meat supply and left them with useful items such as hatchets, knives, sewing needles, boards for sleds, and even a box of soap.

In mid-August they met an American, Harry Whitney, who had spent the year hunting and living in Greenland. Whitney had some disturbing news for the expedition: an American doctor and explorer, Frederick Cook, had recently left Greenland. Cook told Whitney that he had made a successful trip to the North Pole in 1908. Henson and MacMillan interviewed Cook's two Inuit assistants and determined that Cook had never reached the top. Then, rather than rush home to set

Harry Whitney brought disturbing news
to Peary and his crew that Cook was claiming
to have been the first to reach the North Pole.

46

Frederick Cook's journey was later proven not to have reached the North Pole.

the record straight, Peary's expedition stayed in the Arctic to continue hunting for the Inuits' winter food supply.

In late August, they met the schooner *Jeanie*, which was full of coal for the *Roosevelt* and mail for the men. Arriving at Indian Harbor on September 5, the expedition was greeted by cheering crowds. At last, they were able to send home news that their trip was successful and that they would soon be home.

Peary telegraphed the New York Times and Associated Press, saying simply: "Stars and Stripes nailed to the Pole." Henson telegraphed his wife Lucy that when he came home this time, it would be to stay.

CHAPTER SEVEN
A
COLD WELCOME

Instead of the glory he expected upon his return, Peary had to fight for his honor: Frederick Cook sent out telegraphs claiming his success in the Arctic just five days before Peary. Peary called Cook a liar, saying Cook's Inuit assistants denied traveling far enough to reach the pole. Cook responded that he had asked his companions to keep the trip a secret.

Cook was honored by the Danish king and the Royal Danish Geographic Society, and made thousands of dollars on a lecture tour in the United States, where the American public considered Peary a sore loser. When Cook finally gave his expedition records to the University of Copenhagen in Denmark, which had requested them, the university declared the records proved nothing. By then, Cook had left the United States, disappearing from public view.

Eventually, a committee formed by the National Geographic Society decided in Peary's favor after study-

The Cook controversy was the topic of news stories and cartoons around the world.

ing his expedition records. Other explorers familiar with Greenland and its native people threw their support to Peary.

What, in the meantime, was Matt Henson doing after his adventurous years in the Arctic? His wife, certain that Matt would be well paid for his contributions to Peary's success, quit her bank teller's job. But soon she had to ask for it back. While his expedition companions had their professions to return to, Henson's profession was Arctic explorer, and there was no demand for that in New York City. In 1909, black people often found it difficult to find well-paid work no matter where they had been. Having received only $250 for his work on the expedition, Henson took a $16-a-week job as a garage handyman in Brooklyn.

Peary stayed secluded at his Maine home, refusing to discuss his trip until he felt that his claim had been proved. He expected the same conduct from his former assistants. Henson knew this when William Brady, a Broadway producer, approached Matt about a lecture tour. But Henson also needed to earn a decent living. He agreed to let Brady arrange a tour.

Beginning in the Northeast, traveling through the Midwest and finishing in California, Henson spent the next several months describing his Arctic adventures. Nervous at first, he improved as he went along and turned into an entertaining speaker. But often he spoke to small audiences. Perhaps the public had tired of

This formal portrait of Matthew Henson
appeared opposite the title page of his book
A Negro Explorer at the North Pole.

52

hearing about the expedition. Or, maybe because of his race, Henson wasn't taken seriously as an expedition member.

In any case, the tour didn't make much money or help convince the public that Peary and Henson truly were the first men to reach the North Pole. Henson returned home early in 1911 with $2,800, not a great sum but enough to support him while he began another project: writing his book.

He contacted Peary, asking him to write an introduction for his book. Though he'd been angered by Henson's lecture tour, Peary agreed. "The example and experience of Matthew Henson," Peary said in his introduction to *A Negro Explorer at the North Pole*, show that "race, or color, or bringing-up, or environment, count nothing against a determined heart, if it is backed by and aided by intelligence." Peary also wrote several letters for job recommendations for Henson. The book, like Henson's earlier lecture tour, didn't make much money.

Former expedition members Bartlett, Borup, and MacMillan also spoke up for Henson, and other African Americans began honoring him with awards. But Henson still needed a job.

Charles Anderson, a local black politician, wrote to President William Howard Taft and reminded him of the many years Matt had spent helping the United States achieve the honor of reaching the North Pole, and that a government job was the least the country could do to repay him.

So, at age forty-six, Henson became a messenger at the U.S. Customs House in New York, but had to spend Christmas seasons working at the post office as well. He didn't retire until he was seventy years old.

He never received a pension, and forty-five years after the expedition, the government finally awarded Henson and the other expedition members medals for their 1909 achievement in the Arctic. (Peary had died in 1920.)

Organizations weren't much quicker to recognize Henson's achievement. In 1937, he was accepted into the Explorers Club, twenty-eight years after the dash to the pole. In 1938, he became an honorary member of Pittsburgh's Academy of Science and Art. Then, the Geographic Society of Chicago awarded him a gold medal, on the back of which were inscribed the words Peary once used to describe his assistant to MacMillan: "I can't get along without him." In 1954, Matt and Lucy went to Washington D.C., to place a wreath on Peary's grave at Arlington National Cemetery. Afterward, the couple was received at the White House by President Dwight D. Eisenhower.

But, usually, Matt and Lucy led quiet lives in their Harlem neighborhood of New York City. There, Henson was a celebrity, though he didn't talk much anymore about his days in the Arctic — people must get tired of

Henson at work at the
U.S. Customs House in New York City.

*Matthew and Lucy Henson
met President Eisenhower
in the White House.*

hearing about that, he figured. Finally, at age eighty-eight, he suddenly became ill and died shortly after emergency surgery in 1955.

Matthew Henson receives a naval funeral at Arlington National Cemetery in 1988.

But Matthew Henson wasn't forgotten. Elementary schools in Chicago and Baltimore were named after him, as was a university gymnasium in New Orleans. Most notable, perhaps, was the bronze plaque honoring him that was placed in the state capitol building of Maryland, the former slave state where he had been born. Finally, in 1988, Henson's remains were moved to a resting site near Peary's in Arlington National Cemetery, with his new headstone reading "Matthew Alexander Henson. Co-Discoverer of the North Pole." Finally, Henson was reunited with the man who had filled his days with adventure.

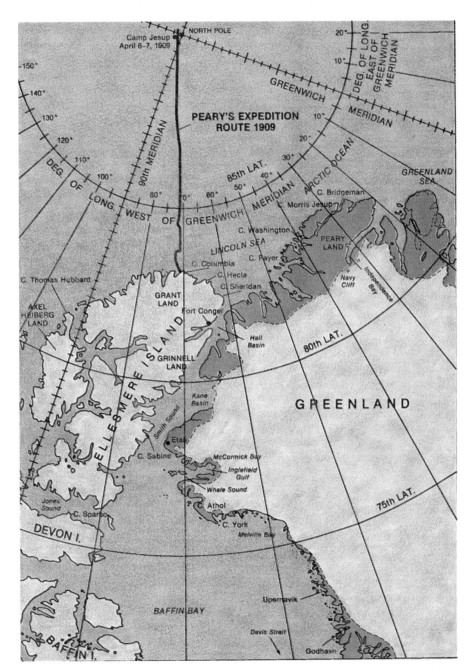

NORTH POLE
Camp Jesup
April 6–7, 1909

PEARY'S EXPEDITION
ROUTE 1909

DEG. OF LONG.
EAST OF
GREENWICH
MERIDIAN

20°
10°

GREENWICH

10°

20°

30°

40°

MERIDIAN

DEG. OF LONG. WEST OF GREENWICH MERIDIAN

85th LAT.

90th MERIDIAN

150°
140°
130°
120°
110°
100°
80°
60°
50°
0°

ARCTIC OCEAN

GREENLAND
SEA

C. Bridgeman
C. Morris Jesup

C. Washington

LINCOLN SEA

PEARY
LAND

C. Thomas Hubbard

C. Columbia
C. Hecla
C. Sheridan

C. Payer

Navy
Cliff

Independence Bay

AXEL
HEIBERG
LAND

GRANT
LAND

Fort Conger

ELLESMERE ISLAND

Hall
Basin

80th LAT.

GRINNELL
LAND

Kane
Basin

GREENLAND

Smith Sound

Etah

C. Sabine

McCormick Bay

Inglefield
Gulf

Whale Sound

Jones
Sound

C. Sparbo

Athol

C. York

Melville Bay

75th LAT.

DEVON I.

BAFFIN BAY

Upernavik

Davis Strait

Godhavn

BAFFIN I.

FOR FURTHER READING

FOR OLDER READERS:

Counter, S. Allen. *North Pole Legacy: Black, White and Eskimo*. Amherst: University of Massachusetts Press, 1991.

Henson, Matthew Alexander. *A Negro Explorer at the North Pole*. New York: Arno Press, 1969.

FOR MIDDLE READERS:

Anderson, Madelyn Klein. *Robert E. Peary and the Fight for the North Pole*. New York: Franklin Watts, 1992.

Dolan, Sean. *Matthew Henson*. New York: Chelsea Juniors, 1992.

Ferris, Jeri. *Arctic Explorer: The Story of Matthew Henson*. Minneapolis: Carolrhoda Books, 1989.

Gilman, Michael. *Matthew Henson*. New York: Chelsea House, 1988.

Gleiter, Jan. *Matthew Henson*. Milwaukee: Raintree Children's Books, 1988.

INDEX

Page numbers in *italics* refer to illustrations.

ABOUT
THE
AUTHOR

Jean Kinney Williams grew up in Ohio and now lives in Maryland with her husband and four children. She studied journalism in college and, in addition to writing, enjoys reading, volunteering at church, and spending time with her family.